BUHARIONOMICS
A Harvest of Assurances

Uwem Essia

DEDICATION

To the hope of a better Nigeria

TABLE OF CONTENTS

PREFACE

Muhammadu Buhari the fifth democratically elected President of Nigeria can be described as an enigma for several good reasons. Firstly he took over power in 1983 from a democratically elected second republic president, Shehu Shagari, in a bloodless coup and was toppled less than two years after in 1985 by his close associate, Ibrahim Babangida. His determination to return to power got him to contest elections as a presidential candidate in 2003, 2007, and 2011. He lost in those three attempts and the frustrated Buhari tearfully announced that the 2011 attempt was his last presidential contest. That was not to be so because in 2015 he contested again as the candidate of the All Progressive Congress (APC) and won. Goodluck Jonathan who claims that his political ambition was not worth the blood of any Nigerian accepted defeat and Muhammadu Buhari was sworn in.

President Buhari's first term (2015 – 2019) was characterized by several misfortunes. Majorly he was sick and hospitalized for some months, to the extent that many believed that he will make history again as a second Katsina State-born President to die in power, the first being late Umaru Yar'Adua. But the enigmatic

Buhari survived and returned looking younger and stronger, even as the conspiracy theory that he has been cloned was rife. While the cloned Buhari story still gains popularity among many Nigerians outside government circles, former President Obasanjo observed angrily recently that the real Buhari couldn't die and a human clone used as the president without people like him knowing.

It is submitted here that the months of sickness, the memories of his 1985 overthrow, and his commitment to pacifying interests in the North impeded performance during his first term (2015 – 2019). Also, the dwindling oil prices which started in 2014 (before his takeover), and his unguarded comments/remarks added up to make his first term a not so delightful experience to many Nigerians.

However, he managed to secure reelection in 2020 and appears to be enjoying better health compared to his first term. He has promised to leave Nigeria better than he met it. He recently labeled the bandits ravaging the North as terrorists and has vowed to crush them alongside other violent extremists.

Similar to the approach adopted more recently by President Biden in the U.S., President Buhari believes he can spend his way out of Nigeria's current recession, using the argument that there is no debt problem but a revenue problem. Hence since 2019, the Buhari administration has been spending heavily on infrastructure development and social welfare programs at a scale that is unprecedented in Nigeria's history. He started late but appears to be in hurry to leave behind legacies.

This book examines Mr. President's performance so far; his success and mistakes, and the political environment of his presidency. Suggestions on how to achieve success faster are also proposed. Mr. President has to turn things around quickly so that the assurances he has been giving Nigerian will not be in vain.

The book has eight chapters. Chapter one conjectures how the president's performance in the first term was seriously impaired by 'the Ghost of the 1985 Coup'. He had to find trusted allies to work with. Chapter two explains how the cabal he worked with significantly influenced his policies and programs, quite often adversely. Chapter three discusses how leading Nigeria is complicated by the heavy influences of ethnicity and corruption. The leaders are under severe pressure to favor clannish and sectional interests. Hence Nigerians have to share the failures of President Buhari and others before him until we change our orientation. Chapter four explains how the unguarded comments of Mr. President contributed to de-marketing Nigeria. Chapter five opines that the unilateral closure of land and sea borders worsened Nigeria's stagflation condition; it caused non-oil exports done informally to neighboring countries through borders to reduce, without significantly reducing the smuggling of rice into Nigeria. Chapter six discusses what can be done to stimulate growth and take the economy out of stagflation. The published achievements of Mr. President as of June 2021 are summarized and analyzed in Chapter seven. Lastly, Chapter eight identifies Mr. President's effort to ensure the fiscal autonomy of State Legislature, State Judiciary, and the Local Government Areas as his most important achievement so far. This effort will further deepen democracy at the grass root and make the State Governors more accountable.

CHAPTER ONE

THE GHOST OF THE 1985 COUP

During his first stay on the saddle of Nigeria's political leadership as a serving general, Muhammadu Buhari was typically a no-nonsense disciplinarian and pragmatic leader who demonstrated zero tolerance for corruption. He sought to make Nigeria self-sufficient and productive. His governance was predicated on practicability, prudent management of available resources, and commitment to meeting pressing needs. Those who dared to dip their hands into the public purse had to pay back and get punished with long jail terms at the same time. He was also known for his civic campaign, named the War Against Indiscipline (WAI), which help as well to accord him charismatic authority.

However, Buhari's military rule lasted for only about two years; a time too short to realistically assess his performance. But currently, in his sixth year as a civilian president, many Nigerians are doubtful if this is the

Buhari they knew. President Buhari appears not to be that no-nonsense anti-corruption crusader and ardent disciplinarian. Although his cult followership is still high in the North, many are disappointed and wondering why he has so changed.

Looking back into his brief stay as a military head of state (1983 – 1985) may provide some insight as to what happened and why he changed. In that regard, it can rightly be said that during that first-coming his success was predicated on the fact that he had very good assistants, especially in the persons of Tunde Idiagbon, the Chief of Staff Supreme Headquarters (his second in command), and Ibrahim Babangida (Chief of Army Staff). The Late Tunde Idiagbon stood in for him effectively as far as day-to-day governance matters were concerned. Fingers point to Tunde Idiagbon as the actor behind the curtains for Buhari during his first coming (1983 – 1985). His diligence, commitment, and dexterity ably converted Buharism into a governance and control tool. But Babangida whom he equally trusted took advantage of him and toppled the government. From the brief narrative above, one can conjecture that during the 1983 – 1985 era, he was willing and ready to work in teams, and cede significant authority to trusted intelligent individuals from any state of the federation who had the demonstrable capacity to deliver. But this openness had to change in his second coming as a civilian president due to the betrayal of Ibrahim Babangida and the other servicemen that connived to topple him. The 1985 ouster experience significantly explains why Muhammadu Buhari, the civilian president, is significantly different from the no-nonsense head of the military junta during 1983 -1985.

That he was unceremoniously pushed out of power was perhaps why he fought to return as civilian president and not necessarily that he had anything new to offer. Also, his cult followership made him a formidable candidate for any party seeking to win a presidential election. Others were willing to sacrifice their money, time, and goodwill to have him contest because of his popularity. Incidentally, when the opportunity he fought for severally finally came in 2015 he surprisingly developed undue coolness. The first sign of this was that it took him nearly six months to form a full cabinet. His dream came true; but he had to take his time since as they say, "once bitten, twice shy." He had to make some hard choices. Firstly since working freely in teams with people failed him during 1983-1985, he had to retreat to form a small inner circle of advisers and trustees using mainly people connected to him by blood. His close relatives are likely to lose if they help to topple him, but stand to gain more if he remains in power. This small group or cabal works largely behind the scenes gathering information and facilitating all the appointments and other major decisions.

Secondly, those to be appointed to sensitive posts have to be reasonably knowledgeable and very trustworthy. Trust has to be prioritized over intelligence because what was needed more was stability and not necessarily speed. Very intelligent people may bring speedy growth but at the cost of instability. Once an appointee is stable and represents a key interest group, he/she had to be kept even where service quality is minimally sacrificed. And, thirdly, carrying along the powerful interest groups especially in the North was necessary for stability and maintaining/growing his cult followership. Having strong followership is considered important because, in the event of another abrupt ouster, which the cabal did not rule out, the cult followers can launch a counter-revolution to return Mr. President to power. Moreover, being a civilian regime it could have been reasoned that measures like War Against Indiscipline (WAI) and price control which were quite effective during his first coming were no longer expedient due to the possibility that they may overheat the polity.

I conjecture that the actions and conduct of Muhammadu Buhari as a civilian president are informed largely by this cabal, many of them old hands and directly related to him. These cabal members may co-opt their close associates into different layers of advisers and jobbers who run the country remotely, albeit some of them have been given political appointments. President Buhari may have chosen to adopt this approach because he is careful to avoid what happened in 1985. At the same time, he has to consolidate his hold on power, perform excellently and leave behind legacies that outlive him, so that he can retain lifelong political relevance in and out of office.

The conjectural framework constructed above may be used to explain some of the events that occur around the Buhari presidency. Consider for instance the relationship between Mr. President and the Vice President, Professor Yemi Osibanjo. The VP I perceive was picked as part of the political bargain within the ruling political party. However, it is possible that Mr. President likes the VP as a person and perhaps would not mind ceding more functions to him. But the cabal may not be very comfortable with that decision because Osibanjo is cerebral and potentially innovative. Recall that during one of his travels for treatment aboard, the VP formally acted for the President and was conspicuous. With his eloquence and ability to speak intelligently on nearly all subjects without reference to pre-written texts, many Nigerian began to see him as a good candidate for president. That was the last time the president allowed him to act formally. Thereafter the president would travel without a formal handing over.

Another area where the ghost of the 1985 ouster can be seen at work is the president's insistence to retain the defense chiefs despite widespread agreement that new service chiefs may bring fresh ideas and energy to the counter-insurgency operation. After all, most of them were due for retirement. Yet it took the president much longer than expected. I guess the ghost of his 1985 ouster could have told him, "work with those you can trust" and the cabal must have equally asked for more time to select their replacement by persons who may never plot or support a coup d'état. Buhari may not personally know the selected persons, but the cabal members will surely do.

On the counter-insurgency/banditry struggle, I guess the cabal may have told him to take it easy and exhaust all possibilities of dialogue. Incidentally, that strategy worked negatively for the state by giving the insurgents sufficient time to institutionalize their strongholds on the society. A similar argument may have been advanced by the cabal for how the herders-farmers conflict should be managed.

Thus it is conjectured here that Buhari's experience as a military head of state who got ousted unceremoniously is largely responsible for how his second coming as a civilian president is characterized. His attempt to protect himself from possible takeover again may explain his penchant for acting with less speed on reforms and retaining some appointees that may perform poorly but their appointment serves to protect some political interests. Without the 1985 ouster experience, I guess President Buhari would have freely brought in more performers into his government. When the focus is stability, and with the ghost of the 1985 ouster still whispering that "you may be toppled again,' the president like any other rational person will need to look before leaping.

CHAPTER TWO

THE INFLUENCE 'OF A FEW PEOPLE'

From all indications the cabal that informs the president's actions, especially during his first term 2015 – 2019 did not appear to be in close league with the first lady, Aisha Buhari who many believe should be the closest person to Mr. President. It is obvious that the cabal related directly to Mr. President, to the extent that at some point during one of those seasons that he had to be hospitalized, it was reported that she was not allowed to see him. If that report is correct, then one may ask, how close could the cabal members be that they were able to hijack Mr. President from his wife and by extension immediate family?

In an interview with Naziru Mikailu from BBC Hausa in 2016, Aisha Buhari said:

"The president does not know 45 out of 50 of the people he appointed and I don't know them either, despite being his wife of 27 years."

She warned further that, "If it continues like this, I'm not going to be part of any [re-election] movement,"

The First Lady's outburst confirms, at least for that material time that President Buhari's government had been hijacked by only a "few people", who were behind presidential appointments. President Buhari was on a visit to Germany where he was confronted with his wife's remarks, and with a chuckle, he responded quite undiplomatically that, "I don't know which party my wife belongs to, but she belongs to my kitchen and my living room and the other room." This poorly reasoned remark attracted a frown from his host, Chancellor Merkel.

The First Lady explained further that people who did not share the vision of the ruling party were now appointed to top posts due to the influence wielded by a "few people." Some of her critics argue however that she had these to say because of being played out in the presidency power tussle. But the question is why should she be played out in the first place? If as a wife of the President she does know what her husband is doing, then how are we sure that Mr. President is not being misled by the cabal? In any case, the First Lady's outburst wielded a severe blow to the tough, no-nonsense posture of the president, and bolstered accusations that his government is influenced by 'a few people', and as well contradicts Mr. President's popular remark during his inauguration that he belongs to nobody.

From all indications, there is a powerful cabal that influences what is happening in the government. However, the First Lady refused to name the cabal members, but advised that "You will know them if you watch television."

I believe that Aisha Buhari has a genuine concern for her husband and would want him to achieve remarkable success as Mr. President. She should not be compared to Jane Appleton Pierce, the wife of Franklin Pierce, 14th president of the U.S. most remembered as the "calamity first lady" who spent her years working against her husband's ambition to be president, and even when he eventually became president continued to attack him. Not so for Aisha, many indeed believe that her active participation in the campaigns leading up to the 2015 elections was what got more women to support her husband's presidential bid. She stood by her husband and appears disappointed by the way things are turning out.

Nigerians certainly expected a lot more from President Buhari considering the energy he put into fighting for the post. In 2011 he was visibly in tears while declining further interest in future presidential elections. At the International Conference Centre, where he rendered a tearful goodbye, in the presence of the party's vice-presidential candidate, Pastor Tunde Bakare, Col. Hameed Ali (retd), and Mallam Nasir el Rufai Nigerians watched him with so much sympathy. This might have explained why they voted overwhelmingly for him when once more he stood for election as the APC presidential candidate in 2015, and he won.

Surprisingly, as if regretting winning the election, four months after his inauguration as Nigeria's fifth democratically elected president, Buhari, during an official visit to South Africa, said he wished he had become president earlier, stressing that age would affect his performance in office. Perhaps the negative confession of Mr. President turned natural forces to work in his disfavor as he was sick for some months thereafter. It is hoped that after the First Lady's outburst that he was held hostage by a cabal, the situation might have changed reasonably in his second term.

CHAPTER THREE

PLAYING ON A BAD TURF

In assessing Mr. President, to be fair, the fact that during his first coming (1983 – 1985) and second coming (2015) he met poor global economic outlook has to be taken into account. During both instances, oil prices fell significantly leading to an economic downturn. In 1983–1985, Buhari introduced economic programs/reforms to move the economy out of the straggle-hold of those he considered to be parasitic political elites and aimed to return power/control of the economy to the authentic entrepreneurs and productive firms. Notably, he rejected the Washington Consensus-inspired IMF credit facilities because of the associated neocolonialist conditionality and rather chose to apply cost-cutting measures and price control to check unnecessary hikes in prices. He refused to devalue the naira because it would further complicate the perverseness of poverty. Rather, he considered curbing the importation of goods deemed unnecessary, curtailing oil theft, and swapping oil for goods like machinery to allow the country to sell above the OPEC quota.

Needless to say, many Nigerians' saw Buhari as a defender of the poor who knew what was needed to get Nigeria developed. His economic diagnosis was revolutionary. His anti-corruption campaigns saw many corrupt public officers in jail. There was widespread optimism that alas Nigeria has found its equivalent of Mao Zedong. Albeit, it is difficult to say if such optimism could have lasted long considering that his government was cut short abruptly.

Hence at inception Buhari's second coming in 2015 was a welcome development to Nigerians across regional and ethnoreligious lines. Many expected to see an emboldened anticorruption agencies work assiduously to investigate corrupt cases and send the culprits to jail. More openness in the handling of recovered loots was equally expected. It was reasoned also that insurgency will be short-lived, and the naira strengthened as round-tripping and other corrupt practices that characterize forex management will die naturally. Also, since Buhari argued strongly during his campaign that oil subsidy was a fraud, people expected the refineries to work optimally and fuel prices reduced. Nigerians commonly believed that their Mao Zedong was back and to revolutionize the country *one hand.*

But after his inauguration, days turned to months and months to years; rather than things getting better, they got worse. Nigerians carried baskets filled with Buhari's assurances, but without significant achievements to show. Garri sellers had to introduce a smaller cup, called the Buhari cup that was different from the older bigger cup that now became Jonathan's cup. The name Buhari soon epitomized hardship, cutting cost, and grappling along the bottom line. Did Buhari lie to Nigerian, or did he underestimate the enormity of what it takes to lead a complex country like Nigeria? Certainly one of these answers must be correct.

But as noted earlier some factors were out of his control in both his first and second coming. He has no control over crude oil prices, and oil revenue is Nigeria's lifeline. For an oil-dependent economy falling oil prices is like a human being taken down by a stroke; the individual is incapacitated and unable to do much. Hence for his three campaign points, namely: (1) end insurgency and ensure security of lives and property; (2) promote economic growth and ensure a stable naira exchange rate; and (3) fight and defeat corruption he couldn't achieve much in his first term (2015 -2019). Incidentally, he was able to win re-election for the second term. But then, tongues wagged that he used the power of incumbency extensively, working through the electoral umpire, the Independent Electoral Commission (INEC), and the security agencies. The broadly held view is that without the support of these institutions he would have lost the 2020 elections. In any case, he won both the elections and the case instituted against his election by the leading opposition party candidate, Atiku Abubakar, conclusively at the Nigerian Supreme Court. But President Buhari certainly knows that he has to do more to redeem the public confidence in his ability to perform, much of which was lost during his first term.

But Nigerians must take responsibility for the successes and failures of their political leaders because rightly or wrongly, it is the citizens that elect their political leaders during elections. President Buhari did not emerge from outer spaces; he is one of us. He was selected out of several other candidates as the Presidential candidate of the All People' Congress (APC). He emerged through a process; the party echelon considered him healthy and qualified to run as a presidential candidate. So APC members have to take responsibility for his successes/failures. Equally the electorate, INEC, and Election Tribunal, and the Supreme Court of Nigeria all participated in his emergence and confirmation as the President of the Federal Republic of Nigeria. Those who voted during the elections and those who did not vote are both responsible and guilty if he performs poorly. So rather than just stop at saying that he could have done better, we must help identify the specific areas of weakness and advice on how he and future presidents can do better.

Moreover, the Buhari of 1983-1985 was younger and more energetic. He was physically and mentally alert and had fewer emotional and health issues. By 2015 he was much older and for some months during the first term (2015 – 2019) was hospitalized abroad. It is almost obvious too that even for the months than he remained in Nigeria, he could have been sick as well. Moreover, as a civilian president, he has more interests and constituencies to be mindful of. The Northern states where he has cult followership is his political base and it is expedient that he deals with the challenge of insurgency/banditry cautiously; let's face it, these are his people and Nigeria is still divided on an ethnoreligious basis.

It can be recalled that he severally criticized his predecessor, President Jonathan for being ruthless with insurgents in the North. He must have wished that the bandits/insurgents heed to his pleas and return to the negotiation table or offer themselves for one form of empowerment program or another. But while that approach might have made significant political and economic sense it was not helpful because trust-building between the government and the insurgents/bandits has remained poor for a long time. However, the bandits took advantage of the delayed action by the government to consolidate and pose a significant threat. Sadly it has taken the administration such a long time to realize that violent extremists are like ruthless monsters who can readily eat up even those who feed them, not minding when and where their next meal will come.

A similar argument may apply to the challenges posed by open grazing. I guess Mr. President having been well-traveled does not see cows grazed along roadsides in London, Casablanca, or Tripoli. I know that none of his children or the children of his close relatives are pastoralists. Not even the most distant relative of any member of his cabal is. So why is having a program to put an end to open grazing and embrace ranching a problem, despite the enormous gains of ranching? Experts have argued that ranching can generate more income than petroleum oil if well harnessed. The meat from ranched cattle is soft, healthier, and more nutritious. Ranched cattle yield better hides and skin for the bags, shoes, and furniture industry. There is also an increased milk supply to feed the value chain of a wide ranch of dairy products. And the dung can be composted for manure and biogas production. The technology for producing grass quickly was demonstrated some time ago by the former Minister for Agriculture, Audu Ogbeh.

Moreover, ranching will offer the pastoralist–herders ample schooling opportunities. We can readily begin with radio-for-education and phone-for-education programs since nearly all of them have radio sets and phones. Then give them solar-powered radios and phones and many of them will start schooling in Hausa, Fulfulde, or other languages that they speak. When they are within ranches where fodder availability is secure, learning will become more interesting. The process will certainly take some time, so start it as soon as possible because pastoralism is dehumanizing and even Governor Masari of Katsina State once declared that it is not Islamic. So why are we still practicing it?

I want to believe that Mr. President and his close associates are well aware of these facts and the sound economics behind them. But I guess sound economics may appear either too costly to the cabal or is politically inexpedient. If the pastoralists suddenly become educated then where will the foot soldiers come from? Where will the servants and cheap labor come from? I can imagine such thoughts go through the minds of the cabal members who sometimes argue that pastoralism is the culture of a people, and yet they and their children are exempted from practicing it. Several interest groups are perhaps benefiting from open grazing, and in a society where politics and parochialism overwhelm economic reasoning, it will take an exceptional national-patriotic drive for a president to ignore the dominant voices in his political constituency.

Mr. President has been criticized for not changing service chiefs even when they reached their retirement ages. And when he decides to replace them and other public official officers occupying "sensitive posts", he will most likely pick their replacements from particular sections of the country. Such practices if statistically significant are not in sync with the extant principles of ensuring federal character in appointments and should be discouraged in their entirety. But we have to look at the larger context to appreciate the thought going on in the President's mind. Nigeria is still a country largely divided along ethnoreligious lines and until that is fixed generally there will still be a problem. Also as noted in an earlier chapter, there is still the ghost of his ouster in 1985, and being human he has to take precautionary measures to prevent a repeat occurrence. A Nigerian President, to be successful, needs to carefully select and retain the people that he/she considers sufficiently loyal. An American president can afford to select the most productive senior officer as military chief because a military takeover is not an issue to worry about. But not so in Nigeria, especially for a president who was overthrown in the past abruptly by close allies.

Thus while it is acceptable that President Buhari may not have performed as many of his supporters expected in some areas, the operational environment has to be taken into account. Even the best player may miss some steps in a rough turf. Nigeria's governance environment is highly politicized, with several competing interests. Finding the optimal mix of interests without hurting some groups can prove very difficult. It was so easy for

President Buhari to criticize GEJ. Like football match spectators, Buhari kicked the ball in the air and jeered while GEJ was on the turf in the middle of the match. As GEJ ended his game, Buhari entered and has perhaps realized that spectators never truly know how the turf is and how difficult it is to win. You have to be in the game to know what it takes to play well and win. The realities of the game are bare-faced when you are in the field playing

The tendency for Nigerian leaders to make mistakes is increased by the fact that most people around them fail to say the truth for fear of losing out of favor. The tendency to condemn corrupt leaders that we are not gaining from is quite high. But when people close to us secure an appointment, we will not mind if they cut corners and engage in illegalities that benefit us at the expense of others. By so doing, we lose the courage to tell them the truth. Blinded by power and the praises and cheers of those eating from them, many of our leaders do not know when their self-interest overwhelms the common good. Accordingly, it will take our collective commitment to truth and the existence of strong institutional deterrence and checks and balances for the right development to take place.

In particular, control institutions like the political parties, the Council of States, the National Executive Council, the Legislature, and other statutory and non-statutory advisory bodies that should influence how the business of government is done have to rise to the occasion. Chief Obasanjo has been doing a good job, by standing up to the truth most of the time, but we need more elderly statesmen to rise and speak out when it is necessary. Chief Obasanjo can look at a sitting president with his koro-koro eyes and say 'Mr. President, on this matter you are wrong.' Nonetheless, I believe Chief Obasanjo will make more impact if he approaches a sitting president with his views rather than resort to the publication of an 'open letter'. I believe that a sitting President will readily grant audience to personalities like Chief Obasanjo if it is requested. Confidential letters are also useful. But open letters should only be used when these friendly approaches fail.

Leadership in a democracy should not be seen or taken as a preserve of those in authority only. The citizens should utilize all available opportunities to give their inputs most peacefully. This is because the impact of what the leaders do, whether good or bad, will affect every member of the polity now or shortly. Making inputs in governance should not translate to insulting leaders. Leaders, like all of us, do not like to be insulted. The truth can be rejected because of how it is said. At the same time praising a non-performing leader does not help governance. Sadly that is what most of us benefiting from those in authority do. So while benefiting from that public officer brother, friend, uncle, son, father, or friend, our mouths are full and we are unable to speak out their faults. But when they are out of the office and are replaced, the fault those we are not benefiting from magnifies, because we are no longer eating. Often it is those who are not eating that turn to social critics, human rights fighters, and pro-democracy activists. But once they are in power or close to those in power, they become praise singers and ready to justify whatever their benefactor does no matter how bad. The fact of the matter is that the change we need must start with us.

CHAPTER FOUR

THE COST OF MISCOMMUNICATION

I agree largely with the group of Nigerians who think that President Buhari means well for Nigeria and Nigerians. But the fact remains that Mr. President is making several costly mistakes, which arise because his handlers are not proactive. This tallies with what the First Lady said that Mr. President may not have known most of his handlers. Nonetheless, since the buck stops on his table, he has to be blamed for not working with the right team in a society with millions of suitable persons.

An area that Mr. President seems to have made the most costly mistakes is making remarks or answering questions. A president or head of a country (however named) is an embodiment of the country and the communication that he/she sends out counts. His comments can influence/determine how the rest of the world takes Nigerians. Hence his comments have to be seasoned with sufficient diplomatic spicing and finesse. Understandably his handlers have a lot of convincing to do since he is their boss, but that is the mark of the job. His media handlers need to work extra hard to transform his public speaking into a communicational asset for the country.

In today's world, perceptions (whether based on truth or falsehood) and expectations (whether realizable or not) are as powerful as reality. Utterances of Mr. President and his body language directly affect the perceptions and expectations of citizens and the current and prospective entrepreneurs. For instance, it is common knowledge that fighting corruption was a key reason why many Nigerians, especially from the low and middle classes, voted for President Buhari. Upon mounting the saddle as President, what needed to be done was to further strengthen the anti-graft institutions and allow them to do their job of investigating alleged corrupt practices, and charging matters to the court of law; not media trials or sensationalizing unproven allegations.

Empirical and theoretical evidences suggest that the executive president embodies the foreign policy of his country. He serves as his country's chief image-maker in the international community. He enters into alliances and agreements with other countries, which may or may not even require legislative approval depending on the regime type. As the embodiment of his country's foreign policy, the actions and utterances of the president – particularly among the members of the international system – determine how the country is perceived internationally. For this reason, the executive president should always be mindful of his speeches and comments abroad to avoid diplomatic gaffes that could potentially misrepresent his country and people. He is expected to pursue with evident gusto those ideas that would promote the international standing of his country and nationals; both at home and in the diaspora.

As Caleb Adebayo rightly opines in an online article titled "Government's High Political Risks", published online on June 9, 2021, political risks remain a huge headache for investors in emerging markets. Before investing in a country, investors do due diligence to ensure that political risks are reasonably low. Where the costs of mitigating or addressing outweigh the benefits, they simply move to another market. He notes that Nigeria's political risks have soared in the last year alone, added to the high corruption levels. The Transparency International 2020 Corruption Perception Index places Nigeria at 149, 74 points below neighboring Ghana. This may in part explain why Nigeria is bypassed by international investors for Ghana. Also, a 2021 Marsh political risk index placed Nigeria's political risk in the range of 6.1 to 8 out of 10, the same category with countries like Iran, Afghanistan, Pakistan, and North Korea. Indeed an Africa Risk-Reward index from 2017 pinpointed political risk in Nigeria at 7.3, a number which would have very likely risen to hit the top of the range indicated by Marsh, with an imminent possibility of crossing into the political risk red zone where we have countries like Syria. Among other risks, nearly all considerations in Nigeria are politicized. Ethnic differences are propagated at all levels of governance, Federal and state governments elect which court order to obey and which not to obey. Moreover, the crime rate has continued to rise with incessant killings, terrorist attacks, kidnappings, and other ills. According to David Bruckmeier, a business intelligence analyst based in London, red tapes, pervasive corruption, multiple taxes/obnoxious levies, and government-business disputes hurt both new and old investments.

At the time GEJ was leaving oil prices began to fall. But he certainly left an economy with appreciable global investment outlook. Diaspora Nigerians and others were pushing investment funds into different sectors. Also with the new weapons acquired, the enlisted mercenaries and effective collaboration with Chadian soldiers and the multinational counterinsurgency taskforce, Boko Haram and bandits in the South West areas of Zamfara State were significantly degraded before the rescheduled elections. Nonetheless, the Buhari administration still inherited a poor electric power situation, poverty, unemployment, and general insecurity from the GEJ. However, these challenges have worsened in the last six years. Agricultural production has further worsened due to the influx of insurgents, bandits, and killer herdsmen into many farm settlements. As Babajide Otitoju says often on TVC Journalist Hangout, an Award-Winning TV discussion program, those who claim that GEJ did not achieve much should 'fear God'.

Faced with falling oil prices and the inherited social, economic, and political challenges, it was expected that Mr. President pays keen attention to having a clear understanding of the issues at stake; to continue with what was working or done correctly, identify where gaps existed and determine how to fill them, and assess what new policies/programs were needed to add significant value. Seeing government as a continuum is both economical and less disruptive, and as well gives investors a reasonable sense of stability. For the Boko Haram insurgency particularly jettisoning the arrangements with the mercenaries and the Chadian forces have proven to be very costly.

At the same time, vibes coming from the Mr. President and the presidency needed to be diplomatically seasoned. Although the ruling party changed, it would have been useful to have GEJ and his Vice attend the formal handover and swearing-in of the new president as a show of continuity. But such wisdom was not brought to bear, and it amounted to a loss for the country from the perspective of global economic outlook. Also delaying to form a government after the inauguration hurt investors' expectations and perceptions as well. Some economists argue that the late start was a prelude to the recession that the country was plunged into later. Many current and prospective investors perceived that Mr. President had no ready governance plan/strategy. When the first-term cabinet was eventually formed, Junaid Mohammed, a Second Republic legislator saw the team as an expensive joke because some of the appointees were already implicated for corruption, and how will corrupt ministers deliver good governance, let alone fight corruption? Junaid Mohammed insisted that President Buhari failed to pick the best hands. This as well amounted to a wrong communication about the economy because it suggest the government was not sincere about fighting corruption.

Even while a government was yet to be fully formed, Mr. President began embarking on trips abroad hoping to woo investors and restore the confidence of the international community in the business prospects in Nigeria. Such trips, albeit quite useful, would have been more rewarding if Mr. President's speeches, comments, and remarks were spiced with marketman diplomacy. But that was not the case. In many instances, he was quick to tell his hosts with presidential authority how corrupt Nigeria was, and how determined he was to probe and jail corrupt officials, and why past administrations were the present problems of the country.

It can be argued that the utterances of Mr. President gave current investors attracted to the country by the GEJ administration, who brought in billions of dollars' worth of investment, reasons to quickly divest from Nigeria because those who facilitated their investment in Nigeria may soon be in jail. Those who concluded investment plans had to cancel because his remarks served as warning signals that the anti-corruption stance of the Buhari administration may render the economy unnecessarily unstable. Ironically, since 2015 no key players of the GEJ administration are being sentenced on corruption charges, and yet the global rating of Nigeria for corruption has been worsening. Perhaps as Junaid Mohammed noted, many persons in the corridors of power are themselves corrupt and as Nigerians would say sarcastically, *dog no de chop dog*.

An ace journalist, Ray Ekpu, wrote an article in the Guardian Newspaper titled "Buhari's Unguarded Tongue" on April 24, 2018. Mr. Ekpu argues that President Buhari doesn't filter his speeches before making them or appreciate the connotative and denotative meanings of the words he uses. All words have meanings and can be subjected to literal or metaphorical interpretations. He cites President Buhari's comments at the Commonwealth Business Forum in the UK as an example. "The forum was meant to promote and celebrate the very best of the Commonwealth to a global audience." But in an answer to a question,

President Buhari said that "more than 60% of the population is below 30, a lot of them haven't been to school and they are claiming that Nigeria is an oil-producing country, therefore, they should sit and do nothing and get housing, healthcare, education free." The comment was unnecessary and damaging coming from Mr. President. Unintendedly, his comment validated the oversimplified and stereotypical profiling of Nigerian youths by some foreigners as criminals and lazy, and it was unfair that Mr. President confirmed it.

If Nigerians are criminals today then certainly we learned it from the advanced countries. I am not sure any Nigerian language has straight translations for drug dealing, scamming, internet fraud, and violent extremism. This simply means that these crimes are alien to us. But assuming it is true that Nigeria was the world's corruption and youth criminality capital, is it the place of our president to announce it? Or will those he is announcing help us to change? The president's role wherever he is in the world is to promote Nigeria's good image, not to balloon the negative stories that already exist about Nigeria.

Again in May 2016, then Britain's Prime Minister, Mr. David Cameron described Nigeria as a fantastically corrupt country. This to say the least qualifies as a diplomatic incidence for which the UK envoy in Nigeria should have been invited for consultation and a formal apology demanded. Many Nigerian were genuinely upset by Cameron's irresponsible and exaggerated remark. But in an interview on Sky News thereafter, Mr. President agreed with Mr. Cameron and did not see a need for an apology.

The fact that the President makes too many controversial statements demonstrates that there is a serious problem with how he communicates. Certainly, his communication handlers are not doing their jobs well. President Buhari does not intentionally want to destroy Nigeria. Granted that he likes to speak with exciting candor. Yet it is the place of his handlers to draw his attention always to how to communicate until he gets used to it. There is a need to always compile possible questions for him and sometimes play the devil's advocate so that his answers can be fine-tuned for best reception by the audience.

The main opposition party, the People's Democratic Party (PDP) at some point issued a statement to the effect that the President's utterances abroad were hurting the country's investment outlook. In particular, the blank labeling of Nigerians and past administrations as corrupt negates the fact that there are millions of honest and hard-working individuals/firms who genuinely earn their wealth. Also announcing to the world that the past governments emptied government coffers and that Nigeria is broke, even with its abundant human and natural resources and a sizeable number of billionaires, sent a wrong signal to those doing or intending to do business with the government and Nigerians.

There is also a challenge with the brazenness and wrong timing of government actions. For example, many Nigerians could have supported the Twitter ban in 2021 if it was originally meant to cause the organization to register in Nigeria, with the concomitant effect of having to get them to pay taxes and employ Nigerians. If Twitter is paying taxes in the U.S., the UK, and other advanced countries and will soon be paying in Ghana, then why not Nigeria? But that was not the case, the demand for Twitter to register as a firm in Nigeria was after it was banned because Mr. President's tweet was pulled down. Banning Twitter for pulling down Mr. President's tweet was wrongly timed and, at the same time amounted to poor diplomacy.

Even if Twitter had to be punished for 'undermining Mr. President', his handlers would have advised on better timing and getting a more cogent reason. For example, a media bill sent for speedy passage by the National Assembly to the effect that all social media organs registered in Nigeria as part of the anti-terrorism strategy could have had a quick sale to the population. On the other hand, NCC as part of its regulatory and control functions can demand that since Twitter, Facebook and others provide some pseudo audiovisual communication services that their services fall somehow under their regulatory ambit. So it could have been a case between NCC and Twitter, whereby the federal Ministry of Information might have served as the mediator. Twitter could have still been chided albeit diplomatically.

The diplomatic approach such as described above may appear longer but is decent and less disruptive. But banning Twitter on account of a private tweet of Mr. President attracted national and international condemnation and placed the country in a bad light, thereby hurting the global perception of the country. After all, President Trump was even barred from using Twitter, and rather than imagine a Twitter ban, his response was to create his social media platform by the name "Truth". Perhaps President Buhari should have considered creating a social media organization that will create new jobs instead of the Twitter ban.

The overall outcome of this avoidable negative publicity of the country by Mr. President and his administration was capital flight. Several diaspora Nigerians and foreign investors who were encouraged to come and invest by the investor-friendly incentives of the GEJ administration lost interest and many divested. It is believed that capital outflow within the early years of President Buhari's administration amounted to about 10 billion US dollars, and hence the perennial dollar shortages and progressive slide in the naira exchange rate.

The CBN's immediate response was a blanket stop in the funding of credit cards, without prior notice, even when the holders had adequate funds in their account. Many people in hotels abroad could not make payments because their cards did not deliver cash anymore. Such half measures and shortcuts to solving serious structural problems often backfire and become counterproductive. In this instance, the non-funding of credit cards caused further loss of confidence and continued depreciation of the naira. Rather than reduce the demand for dollars, more Nigerians became anxious to convert their naira to dollar balances at whatever exchange rate. With the scarcity of the dollar becoming more severe, even children schooling abroad couldn't return to school. Small scale businesses were worst hit and the country was plunged into an economic mess that it is still struggling to recover from.

However, it appears that something is being done about it recently because Mr. President's utterances are becoming favorable. A report by the Punch newspaper of November 12 2021 prepared by Segun Adewole indicates that Mr. President's comments about Nigerians are showing significant improvement in recent times. President Buhari was reported as saying that the competitiveness which Nigerians display abroad is a result of the good education they acquired before traveling out of the country. This is as he urged Nigerians in Diaspora to always abide by the rules of their host countries. The President said this when he met with the Minister of State Foreign Affairs of the United Arab Emirates, Shaikh Shakboot Alnahyan, at the sidelines of the Paris Peace Forum. Mr. President noted further that Nigerians are everywhere, and their competitiveness starts from home, where they have acquired a good education, gone into businesses, and then take all that abroad." More of such kind commentaries from Mr. President is needed to enhance the country's investment outlook.

CHAPTER FIVE

FUTILITY OF BORDER CLOSURE

Many analysts believe that border closure under President Buhari has not yielded the desired purpose, but rather helped to worsen the situation. In particular, the continued cross-border smuggling raises questions about the strategy's effectiveness and the real reasons behind it. At the same time, consideration was not given to the fact that a substantial chunk of Nigeria's non-oil exports destined for many Sub-Saharan African countries is done through the land/sea borders, and keeping them closed have contributed to the scarcity of foreign exchange because informal non-oil exports have reduced significantly. Our refurbished automobile engines and other automotive parts and accessories, consumable manufactures, domestic/industrial electrical materials, plumbing fittings and water storage tanks, and lighting, fabrics, pasta, footwear and bags, palm oil, groundnuts, traditional herbal medicines, and so on pass through our land and sea borders to reach nearly all the West African coastal countries, up to Senegal and even Morocco, and down to the southern African countries such as Mozambique, Angola, Namibia, and Zimbabwe.

More seriously, the border closure fails to take into account the fact that Nigerian entrepreneurs have significant shares in the economies of many SSA countries. Take Cameroon for instance, Dangote dominates cement production significantly. And ironically the foreign rice being smuggled from Cameroon to Nigeria is bulk-purchased into Cameroon and re-bagged for sale there by a firm reportedly owned by Dangote. At the same time businesses in the areas of knockdown motor vehicle engines and parts, cosmetics, shoes and bags, pharmaceuticals, and several other sectors within the Cameroonian economy are dominated by Nigerians. I guess the same apply to Benin Republic, Niger, Chad, Gabon, Sao Tome, and Equatorial Guinea.

Thus policies of the Nigerian government that aim directly or indirectly to hurt our neighboring countries turn around to hurt Nigerians more. For example, nearly all the boats ferrying goods and persons between Cameroon and Nigeria are owned and operated by Nigerians, and when they stop moving hundreds of Nigerians become unemployed. Therefore while designing trade policies, the large number of Nigerians settled and doing businesses in other countries should be taken into consideration. When it is considered that Nigerians have a significant economic presence and stakes in many of our neighboring countries' economies, it becomes obvious that ultimately trading with those countries benefits us more.

If informal trade in properly estimated and taken into consideration, it can be argued that Nigeria's actual Gross National Product (GNP) far exceeds what is reported formally. Moreover, our GNP (the value of goods and services produced by Nigerians in and outside Nigeria) is far larger than our GDP (the value of goods/services produced in Nigeria), We may consider identifying the gap between the GNP and the GDP as the value of goods and services produced by Nigerians outside Nigeria, which can be described as the Gross External Product (GEP). When consideration is given to the GEP, then it will be obvious that the border closure is at best shortsighted, ill-conceived, and an avoidable mistake. It certainly amounts to Nigeria shooting itself on the foot.

If the aim was to check the smuggling of rice into Nigeria, then it failed as far as southern Cameroon – Nigeria border is concerned because thousands of tons of Dangote rice is moved almost hourly through old and newly created smuggling routes connecting Cameroon and Nigeria. Even undergraduate students of international trade know that direct measures can't successfully enforce trade restrictions even in the most advanced countries. Rather they exacerbate corruption and the creation of more smuggling routes. However, win-win negotiations with neighboring countries will always work better than unilateral actions.

Besides a growing number of Nigerians prefer to consume local rice because it is believed to be more nourishing. All that is needed to strengthen the consumption of local rice is to invest in the improvement of its production, processing and packaging, and marketing. Growth in the local production of any good sustained by forcefully restricting the supply of a perceived substitute may cause some short-term increase in production of the local good initially but not for long because the increase was not stimulated by improvements in either productivity, processing, or marketing. We have to stop the unnecessary suffering and cost associated with several years of enforcing an impossible ban on what we love to consume.

Thus it is recommended here that the importation of rice be legitimized but with a tariff level that on the one hand reasonably protects the local producer, and on the other hand, renders smuggling rice into the country unattractive. After all, the firm processing/packaging a significant quantity of rice into Nigeria from Cameroon is our own Dangote, who is doing a legitimate business in

Cameroon that employs some Nigerians who send remittances back home.

Moreover, the federal government must take trade diplomacy more seriously. Note that although Nigeria announced a unilateral partial reopening of its land and sea borders between December 2020 and January 2021, the Cameroonian Government has refused to formally open its border perhaps as tit for tat for Nigeria's unilateral closure. So while traveling across both countries continues, passports are not stamped and the relevant charges and customs duties end up in the pockets of the security operatives on both sides. The unilateral border closure and opening are certainly avoidable mistakes. Nigeria is undoubtedly a big country, but we need all our neighbors more than they need us because Nigerians entrepreneurs control significant shares of the commanding heights of the economies of most neighboring countries. Our citizens own residential estates, universities, industries, and so on in these countries, far more than their citizens own within Nigeria.

Ironically as military head of state, Muhammadu Buhari imposed similar border closures in 1984, which failed to achieve the desired result. The 2019 border closure I guess was the governments' attempt to wedge the country against dumping that was anticipated following Nigeria's reluctant ratification of the African Continental

Free Trade Area (AfCFTA) Agreement. It was anticipated that the agreement would allow external suppliers from nearby African countries to capture much of the Nigerian and regional markets. Such expectations were ill-thought because many of the big economic players in the neighboring countries are either of Nigerian origin or are seriously linked to Nigerians, and ultimately a greater share of the proceeds from such businesses, if successful end up in the pockets of Nigerians, one way or the other.

Rather than close borders, Nigeria as a leading beneficiary of pan-African trade and cooperation should grow a win-win cooperative relationship with its neighbors. Together Nigeria and its neighbors can invest in rural development, improving border security and intelligence sharing, tackling corruption among border officials, and correcting economic policies that allow smuggling, rather than adopt measures that are not just difficult to implement, but as well having a far-reaching adverse impact on non-oil exports and the transnational businesses of many Nigerians living and doing business outside Nigeria.

Accordingly, the present government's effort to reinvent the failed protectionist measures that Buhari adopted during his first coming, which even then stifled the economy has contributed to our present economic woes. The protectionist stance of the present government is engendering capital flight and leading to a hike in prices, and making smuggling even more lucrative (thus causing significant loss in the revenue that could have been earned as customs duties. Rather than direct restrictions and bans, reforming our ports and engaging producers/importers may be better ways to go. Using quick solutions to solve deeper problems has not worked anywhere. But easing the number of processes and cost of clearing goods in our ports will significantly help. The use of sophisticated scanners to examine the content of containers will help also.

Understandably the Nigerian customs have praised the border closure policy perhaps because a good number of them cart home gifts of money and smuggled goods daily. This hypocrisy is what may kill our economy if allowed to continue. In any case, the official argument of the Nigerian customs is first that the border closure is an inevitable step to curtail the inflows of illegal goods into the country. Secondly, the border closure will prevent the dumping of agricultural and industrial products, and thereby protect local producers from cheaper imported substitutes for the commodities they produce.

For the first argument as discussed above, the border control has increased the number of smuggling routes without actually reducing the smuggled imports of rice, particularly. But it has reduced our exports that are smuggled to our neighboring countries. So rather than fight the cross-flow of smuggled goods, a more realistic option is to review what is making smuggling thrive and find ways to internalize the economies. For example, finished petroleum produce – petrol and diesel mainly – are smuggled out of Nigeria to neighboring countries where their pump prices are far higher in naira terms. So rather than fighting the smuggling, we can quicken the construction of local refineries and legitimize the export of finished petroleum products. Smuggling can only be ended or outgrown when the underlying causes are treated. Outright bans if ever successful will be achieved at higher costs.

People will always find ways to flout border restrictions and engage in trade whenever it is beneficial to do so regardless of the barriers. Closing the official borders will naturally hurt legitimate businesses/traveling but improve the ingenuity and cleverness of smugglers. Take the Ekok-Mfum border for instance, when the official border was closed and people were not allowed to walk across, fishermen found it more profitable to abandon fishing for the quick business of ferrying persons and goods across the boundary (river) between the two countries. Security operatives and customs officials of both countries are on either side collecting monies that certainly do not enter the purses for their respective countries. Even when the borders get open, the newly created smuggling routes may never be closed, but continue to serve the purposes of trafficking illicit drugs, arms, and human beings.

Smuggling occurs through several illegal routes, often in collaboration with corrupt customs officials and a ban on smuggled goods increases the illegitimate earnings of the customs and other security operatives working at the borders. The adverse consequences of the border closure are far-reaching. Food inflation rose to about 15 percent in November 2019, the highest in several years, according to the National Bureau of Statistics. Also, over 2.6 million Nigerians became food insecure, especially in the Northeast with the concomitant effect of growing the Boko Haram insurgency. Undisputedly, border closures cannot replace more serious efforts to improve domestic capacity and avoid unnecessary tensions with our neighbors.

CHAPTER SIX

GROWING THE ECONOMY

Economists define stagflation as a period of slow economic growth, a high unemployment rate, and higher inflation. It is an intractable economic malfunction that exacerbates poverty, insecurity, and state fragility, and an early escape from it may be very difficult. The National Bureau of Statistics (NBS) reported that Nigeria barely slipped out of a recession in the 4th quarter of 2020 with a 0.11 percent GDP Growth rate. Although a welcome development, it is the slowest GDP Growth rate recorded for any quarter since 2011. The NBS revealed also that the Inflation rate spiked up to 16.47 percent, the highest since April 2017. But Nigeria's GDP per quarter has averaged only 0.18 percent in the last 6 years. More pathetic is the fact that the Buhari government has presided over a consumer price index change of 108.6 percent, implying that in the last 6 years prices of nearly every good have at least doubled. Invariably whatever gain there is that came from the very minimal growth in productivity was lost to inflation. Without a doubt,

Nigeria is in a protracted state of stagflation, and it has been so since the Buhari administration came into power in 2015.

Incidentally, the situation was not quite different during his first coming (1983 – 1985). Nigeria's GDP Growth rate for 1983 and 1984 was -10.92 percent and -1.12 percent respectively. The annual inflation rate in the same period was 17.2 percent and 23.8 percent respectively. So are we right to say that Buharinomics is synonymous with Stagflation? One may argue otherwise that the correspondence in the economic situations now and during his first coming are coincidences. After all, Muhammadu Buhari as a person cannot alter oil prices, which is a key factor that determines the state of our earnings, given the high dependency of our economy on crude oil. Moreover, the price of crude oil began to fall in 2014.

Still, a cocktail of poorly thought-out policies can be blamed for the economic downturn experienced during the Buhari presidency since 2015. Firstly is excessive borrowing, ostensibly for the government to spend its way out of the recession. The economics behind this is similar to what is now commonly referred to as Bidenomics, whereby the Biden – Harris American administration has planned to spend a whopping 3 trillion US dollars on Infrastructure development and pro-poor subsidies. Thus as concerning spending to take the economy out of recession, there are striking parallels for Buharionomics and Bidenonics. The difference for Nigeria perhaps is what the loaned funds would be spent on and how the cost of debt servicing will impact ongoing development activities.

Economists agree generally that borrowed funds committed to projects that can yield returns or generate new activities that will yield returns through its linkages and integration effects are beneficial to development and increase the likelihood that the loans are repaid on schedule and don't pose a significant intergenerational debt burden. At the same time, a challenging situation that may significantly reduce the possible gain from spending out of a recession is the high import dependence of the intended infrastructure development efforts. For Bidenomics, a significant proportion of the human and material resources to be used for the massive infrastructural development will come from within the American economy. But for Buharionomics a larger share of the machinery and other inputs, and even the construction firms will be sourced externally. Hence for Buharionomics, further capital accumulation will have a high import component. With a depreciating naira, the domestic inflation rate may continue to increase. At the same time, the component of the deficit to be financed through domestic borrowing will cause a further hike in the rate of interest and crowd out micro and small enterprises who may not be able to secure affordable credit from the domestic money and capital markets.

Additionally, the stagflation experienced in the economy has significantly affected domestic purchasing power, such that even where local firms find resources to produce more, selling in the domestic market will be challenging because of a deficiency in aggregate demand. The situation of micro/small businesses is complicated further by their inability to expand their market through informal cross-border trade channels that the obnoxious border closure due to the obnoxious border closure.

The Way Forward

A comprehensive rethink of the current approach of the Nigerian government to various issues should be considered. Firstly, vowing to crush bandits/insurgents/killer herdsmen is a welcome development and should be implemented expeditiously because spending the economy out of recession may amount to nothing if violent extremism in any part of the country continues unabated. Hence other rebellious movements that fail to embrace dialogue for whatever reason should similarly be crushed.

Secondly, the idea of tracing colonial cattle routes may generate a new round of conflict and should be jettisoned. Particularly, it is unconstitutional because the extant land use law gives the authority of legitimizing land rights to the state governor, and attempting to amend it now to enforce the grazing route recovery will be an avoidable vexation of the polity. The path of peace is to place a future deadline for the full ban of open grazing, while livestock cooperatives and guilds all over the country are supported with grant-in-loans to help the acquire lands privately and develop ranches. A modernized livestock sector will grow the beef, leather, and dairy products' value chains significantly to national self-sufficiency and then for exports. This is added to the new jobs to be created, and opportunities for the pastoralists to be educated.

Thirdly, concrete steps should be taken to reduce the cost of doing business in Nigeria. Particularly, the lead time to clearing import or export, and the logistic processes of post-harvest management should be eased or streamlined. Also reducing taxes, and eliminating corrupt practices and obnoxious levies are essential. Equally the power and influence of unions should be curtailed to ensure that it does not impinge on the cost of doing business. No agency, group, or association should be allowed to hold the state to ransom for whatever reason.

Fourthly, existing startup support programs should be expanded and new ones introduced to cover more prospective awardees. The entry-level for the startup programs should be reduced to secondary school graduates so that those who for whatever reason are unable to continue schooling to the university level can enroll in an apprenticeship scheme that is supported by the government. Also, rather than put so much money on one-off direct cash transfers, the government should invest more in building the capacity of young people to be productive as early as possible. A program can be arranged for the apprentices to continue schooling thereafter.

Fifthly, it has become increasingly important that we take checking our population growth seriously, by intensifying family planning and considering amendments to our extant laws on abortion to allow for legal abortion on economic grounds. Given that our social welfare programs are weak and poorly funded, citizens should be allowed to abort pregnancies that can't be catered for. Equally, massive public enlightenment programs should be put in place to encourage safe sex practices and having the number of children that can be cared for.

Sixthly, we must take a closer look at our education system to ensure major reforms. The issue should not just be about paying the teachers/lecturers more, but also ensuring an increase in productivity. Our public education system is getting excessively politicized such that real productivity is being displaced by politics. Right from crèche to the tertiary level, parents prefer enrolling their children in private schools because more teaching is taking place there. Hence, a public-private-civil society governance model should be considered for our education system where the boards of public institutions are rendered autonomous and made to run on a business model, and government places the pupil/students on scholarship/bursary awards. At the tertiary level, the government should as well provide grants for science & technology (S&T) and research and development (R&D) growth. Under this model, the universities can source funding for their development/investment from the capital/money market like other going concerns. The National Universities Commission (NUC) will continue with its regulatory and control functions, and ensure standardization of salaries, curriculum, teaching methods and quality, and teaching/learning conditions.

Seventhly, to ease access to affordable credit by micro and small enterprises given the high cost of borrowing from the domestic banking system, the government can borrow on their behalf offshore and lodge it in the CBN from where the commercial banks can access and lend to micro and small enterprises at very low-interest rates. Funds sourced offshore at 2 to 4 percent can for instance be loaned to producing firms at say 5 to 6 percent for business expansion.

Eighthly, all Nigeria's land and sea borders should be opened after effective dialogue/negotiations with our neighboring countries. Except for arms and ammunition, and illicit drugs that are highly prohibited, legitimate importation of needed goods should be allowed, and the relevant tariffs set to make smuggling unattractive. It should be possible to adjust the tariff from time to time to ensure that domestic production is protected without necessarily making the sectors uncompetitive. And ninthly, given the rising debt stock and growing cost of debt servicing, it is necessary to explore non-debt avenues to finance projects, especially public-private partnership (PPP), and growing direct foreign investment.

CHAPTER SEVEN

ANALYSES OF ACHIEVEMENTS

The Buhari Administration has published a cocktail of landmark achievements that it has recorded. A selected few in the areas of infrastructure development, finance, education, healthcare, sports, anti-corruption, human development, housing, oil and gas, and foreign relations, among others are presented and analyzed in this Chapter.

INFRASTRUCTURE

A1. Creation of an Institutional framework for Infrastructure development

- A special corporation, InfraCo, intended as a world-class Infrastructure development special purpose vehicle with a combined debt and equity take-off capital of N15 trillion. InfraCo is to be managed by an independent infrastructure fund manager. Also, the

Presidential Infrastructure Development Fund (PDF) was established in 2020 with more than $1 billion initial funding.

- InfraCo Plc is a novel development, but it is not exactly clear how the Nigerian National Petroleum Cooperation (NNPC) will be directly involved with road construction, and what the role of the Federal Ministry of Works will be.

A2. *Nigeria Innovation Fund was launched by the NSIA to address investment opportunities in the domestic technology sector*

- The National Information Fund (NIF) will support data networking, data centers, software, Agri-tech, and Bio-tech, and so on. Using this Fund to support hi-tech startups, and grow their connectedness to the primary and secondary sectors of the economy will enhance speedy success.

A3. *So far no government since independence has invested in rail as President Buhari*

- 156km Lagos-Ibadan Standard Gauge Rail;
- Completed the 327km Itakpe-Warri Standard Gauge Rail started 33 years ago;
- Abuja Light Rail completed in 2018;

- Initiated construction of Kano-Maradi Standard Gauge Rail, and revamp of Port-Harcourt-Maiduguri Narrow Gauge Rail;
- Plans concluded for Ibadan-Kano Standard Gauge Rail and the Coastal Rail projects.

A4. Several Road construction projects are ongoing in nearly all parts of the country

- Presidential Infrastructure Development Fund (PIDF), investing over a billion dollars in roads/bridges construction;
- Highway Development and Management Initiative (HDMI) - a PPP program to mobilize trillions of naira in private investment for road repair and maintenance;
- Funds raised from Sukuk Bond since 2017 for road construction/repair projects nationwide.

A5. Massive ports' infrastructure development and upgrading ongoing

- New Terminals for International Airports in Lagos, Abuja, Kano, and Port Harcourt completed as well as the construction of new runway for Abuja and Enugu International Airports. Presidential approval was given for four International Airports to be made Special Economic Zones - Lagos, Kano, Abuja, and Port Harcourt.

- Business activities in dormant Eastern seaports of Calabar, Warri, and Port Harcourt increased. And a new deep seaport approved for Akwa Ibom State.

A6. Development of clean energy infrastructure enhanced nationwide

- *Energizing Education Program* is supporting tertiary health and educational institutions with renewal (solar and gas) energy.
- *Energizing Economies Program is t*aking clean and reliable energy (Solar and Gas) to markets across the country.
- *Solar Power Naija to deliver* 5 million off-grid solar connections to Nigerian households. The Rural Electrification Agency plans to deploy solar-powered grids to Primary Health Centres (PHC) and Unity Schools nationwide.
- *Presidential Power Initiative (PPI), aka Siemens Power Program* - involving the Governments of Nigeria and Germany, and Siemens AG of Germany, to upgrade and modernize Nigeria's electricity grid under the presidential power initiative.

A7. Affordable housing projects facilitated by the federal government ongoing nationwide

- *The Family Homes Fund Limited (FHFL)* - incorporated in September 2016 to implement the National Social Housing scheme. The CBN has allocated a N200 Billion financing facility, with a guarantee by the FGN.

A8. The decade of Gas has been declared by the federal government.

- Ajaokuta-Kaduna-Kano Gas pipeline project ongoing;
- Successful completion of Nigeria's first Marginal Field Bid Round in almost 20 years. It is hoped that a new fiesta of indigenous investment in oil and gas will be open.
- Nigeria and Morocco signed an agreement to develop a US$1.4 billion multipurpose industrial platform (Ammonia and Di-Ammonium Phosphate production plants) using Nigerian gas and Moroccan phosphate to produce 750,000 tons of ammonia and 1 million tons of phosphate fertilizers annually by 2025. It will be located in Ikot-Abasi, Akwa-Ibom State.
- The new NPDC Integrated Gas Handling Facility in Edo State, the largest onshore LPG plant in the country, with a processing capacity of 100 million standard cubic feet of gas daily, was commissioned. ·
- Establishment of a $350m Nigerian Content Intervention Fund, to finance manufacturing, contracts, and assets in the oil and gas industry

- Methanol and other gas processing plants established by NNPC as joint venture projects.
- Policy, Regulatory and Funding Support for the establishment of Modular Refineries across the Niger Delta.
- Launch of the Nigerian Upstream Cost Optimization Programme (NUCOP), to reduce operating expenses through process enhancement and industry collaboration.

A9. A wide range of agricultural support initiatives and programs

- Anchor Borrowers Program (ABP), hosted by the CBN to provide more than 300 billion Naira to millions of smallholder farmers.
- Special-Agro Industrial Processing Zones (SAPZ) Program – to be established across the country, and provided with basic infrastructure such as water, electricity, and roads as well as facilities for skills training.
- *The Green Imperative* – a Nigeria-Brazil Agricultural Mechanization Program aimed at boosting agricultural production in Nigeria.

A10. A Cocktail of Social Investment, Empowerment, and Poverty Alleviation Provided.

- National Social Investment Program – launched in 2016 and is currently the largest such program in

Africa with a National Social Register of poor and vulnerable Nigerians (NSR) having 32.6 million persons from more than 7 million poor and vulnerable households, identified across 708 local government areas.

- Micro-Pension Scheme – Launched in January 2019, to allow self-employed persons and persons working in organizations with less than 3 employees to save for the provision of pension at retirement or incapacitation.

· A cocktail of other targeted Funds anchored by the CBN.

A11. Massive Infrastructural Investments in the Education and Health Sectors.

- Over N1.7 trillion capital intervention to Nigeria's tertiary institutions, through several channels.
- Launch of the Alternate School Programme (ASP), designed to ensure that every out-of-school child in Nigeria gains access to quality basic education, irrespective of social, cultural, or economic circumstance, in line with the aspirations of Sustainable Development Goal 4 (SDG-4).
- Presidential approval for the establishment of the following:
  - Federal Maritime University, in Delta State
  - Nigerian Army University, in Borno State

- Six new Colleges of Education (one per geopolitical zone)
- Six new Federal Polytechnics one per geopolitical zone;
- 6 Federal Science & Technical Colleges (FSTC) were established in 2020 under the phased implementation of the National Youth Policy;
- Tertiary Healthcare Upgrade Programme: Many key Federal Hospitals across the country are being upgraded to effectively manage cancer and other major health challenges.
- Nigeria Sovereign Investment Authority (NSIA) in March 2018 invested US$10m to establish world-class Cancer Treatment Centers in some states.

B. CREATIVE INDUSTRY AND SPORTS

B1. *Support for youth development*

- Establishment of the 75 billion Naira National Youth Investment Fund (NYIF), and the Creative Industry Financing Initiative (CIFI) was established by the CBN in collaboration with the Bankers' Committee
- Handover of the National Theatre, Lagos, to the CBN and the Bankers Committee, for redevelopment into a world-class Creative Park serving the theatre, film, fashion, music, and ICT sectors.

C. FISCAL, TRADE, MONETARY, AND

INVESTMENT REFORMS

C1. Incentivizing investment

- The Nigerian Investment Promotion Council (NIPC) in 2017 completed a long-overdue revision of the list of activities that can benefit from Nigeria's Pioneer Status Incentive, which grants beneficiary companies a 3 to 5-year tax holiday, expanding the tax holiday incentives to qualifying companies in E-commerce, Software Development, Animation, Music, Film and TV.

- Launch of a Visa-on-Arrival Policy, as part of Ease of Doing Business Reforms. In addition, a comprehensive reform of the existing Visa Regime, leading to the rollout in 2020 of a new and enhanced Visa Policy for Nigeria;

Remarks

On Infrastructure Development

- Cost recovery principle should be adopted for all the roads that are to be constructed via the InfraCo, using toll gates and weighbridges. The cost recovery principle should equally apply to other infrastructures. This will ensure that routine maintenance does not become a major burden as is the case now.

- Increasing the supply of electricity for households and industrial use should be prioritized. A particular unit of InfraCo may need to be created for that. Particular attention should be paid to ensuring accessibility and affordability of the technology, equipment, and spares for alternative energy supply for households and used by low energy micro and small businesses. Newer building designs and methods that incorporate spaces for the use of solar, wind, and biogas should be developed and the practitioner adequately trained.

- Local production of alternative energy equipment and spares should be promoted. Also, bottlenecks and sabotages placed on the path of attaining steady electricity supply by the cartels benefiting from the epileptic power supply should be investigated, identified, and removed.

- For inclusive, nationwide, infrastructural development, InfraCo Plc should operate within a framework where it works in league with the relevant ministries in the states responsible for developing or servicing the infrastructures. The state should as well build in the infrastructure needs of its LGAs. Doing so is necessary for the inclusive development of infrastructures in the federation. Besides huge economies of scale may arise from synchronizing the federal, state, and LGA infrastructure development. Co-funding and co-management will be possible and duplications eliminated. At the same time, fair charging for toll gates and weighbridges and equitable revenue sharing of proceeds to all the tiers of the federation will be possible.

On poverty alleviation and empowerment programs

- The resources allocated to empowerment and poverty reduction programs are commendable. But the programs are so many, and the risk that much of the allocated funds will be spent on servicing the multiple administrative structures is high. Tracking/monitoring for value-for-money will equally pose challenges. Pulling together the funds into at most two grand projects that are implemented collaboratively with the states and local government councils is likely to be more impactful.

On the creation of new universities and colleges

- Education is essential for development. But it is important at this stage to prioritize the new institutions being developed, given that there are already several universities, colleges of education, polytechnics, and colleges that are yet to be developed/utilized. What ought to have been prioritized now are dual-use (military and civilian) specialized training tertiary institutions to strengthen growth in hi-tech activity areas like software programming, big data analytics, emergency management, herbal medicine research and production, automotive machinery production (air, land, and sea), and the manufacture of renewal energy equipment and spares, among others.

On youth and Sports Development

- Ongoing investment in the youth and sports development sectors is commendable. But as noted for infrastructures, the use of PPP and inter-government collaboration should be emphasized. For instance, the LGAs working with village/town committees can be supported to create community sports/games centers or parks in close vicinity to communities. Such locations are the birthplaces of international stars. Also, a coordinated program can be put in place to help our talented youths professionalize and travel out.

- Investing in the proliferation of training institutions for vocations like music, artwork/drawing, sculpturing, stone carving, acting, modeling, fashion designing, and photography should be encouraged right from the level of LGAs.

- The federal government should build a fund for youth development along the lines discussed above, and partner with the programs of the states/LGAs through counterpart funding for nationally conceived projects that they have successfully commenced implementation. The multi-layered interventions will again make tracking easier and compel the lowers tiers of government to contribute to the success of the project.

On Trade and Investment Promotion

- To place a higher premium on promoting trade and investment, our embassies/high commissions, and consular services should shift from the conventional armchair political diplomacy to engaging in commercial diplomacies, such as helping Nigerians wanting to do business in their host countries with information, and advisory and facilitation services, and do likewise for the people of the host countries that want to do business in Nigeria. It will be okay even if some of such support services attract minimal charges.

CHAPTER EIGHT
DEEPENING DEMOCRACY

President Buhari has demonstrated serious commitment to ensuring good governance at the level of the federating states and the LGAs. Many Nigerians blame the federal government for nearly all the failures, not minding the fact the federal government takes just about a half of the revenue mobilized monthly. The other half goes to the states and the LGAs. Most Nigerians forget that by the Nigerian constitution, state Governors are the Heads of their respective states and control huge financial, material, and human resources.

Mr. President in 2020 signed an Executive Order that grants financial autonomy to the legislature and the judiciary across the 36 states of the country. The order mandates the Accountant-General of the federation to deduct from source amounts due to state legislatures and judiciaries from the monthly allocation and pay directly to the financial heads of the legislature and judiciary of the states where the Governor refuses to voluntarily implement the Executive Order. The Attorney General of the Federation, Mr. Malami said that Executive Order No. 10 of 2020, made it mandatory that all states of the federation include the allocations of both the legislature and the judiciary in the first-line charge of their budgets. He said consideration was given to all other applicable laws, instruments, conventions, and regulations that provided for financial autonomy at the states.

As the Attorney General rightly noted, implementation of the Executive Order will strengthen the democratic practices at the level of states, make the Governors more accountable, and render the Legislature and Judiciary in the states independent and accountable in line with the tenets of democracy as enshrined in the Nigerian Constitution. He submits that Executive Order 10 derives from the powers vested on the President under Section 5 of the 1999 Constitution (as amended), which extends to the execution and maintenance of the Constitution, laws made by the National Assembly (including but not limited to Section 121(3) of the 1999 Constitution (as amended), which guarantee financial autonomy of the state legislature and state judiciary.

Also in May 2020, Mr. President signed an Executive Order granting outright financial autonomy to the local government councils, as the third tier of government as provided for in the 1999 Constitution (As Amended).

This will remain one of the landmark achievements of this administration because hitherto the local government system has been tossed around by state governors and the state legislatures. By this courage, President Buhari has demonstrated capacity for shifting the paradigm at the sub-national level from what appeared to be the autocracy of the governor, towards a more people-friendly leadership structure where the three tiers of government operate as partners respecting each other's boundaries without one having to lord over the other.

It can be said unequivocally that since 1999 no other President has taken such a bold step as President Buhari has done to deepen democratic governance and promote transparency and accountability at the lower level of governance. In any case, the executive order is in sync with existing constitutional provisions. However, the Governors have been using other seemingly contradicting provisions of the constitution to circumvent granting autonomy to the legislature and judiciary, and the LGAs. In particular, the LGAs are recognized as a tier of government in Section 7 of the Constitution. But the State Governors readily exploit the requirement of having to operate/supervise the joint state-LGA account, as well as the power granted the state legislative powers to make laws for the good governance of the local governments to turn the LGAs to their whipping horses, and thus superimpose an autocracy at the grassroots within a federal democracy.

With the financial autonomy granted to the LGAs, it now amounts to misappropriation for a Governor to misallocate the LGA funds for other purposes. At the same time, the LGA chairpersons will be held accountable for the funds that they approve for use by the Governors without cogent explanation. It is not yet Uhuru because old habits take time to change, but this is certainly one great step that President Buhari has taken well.

Expectedly the Governors who have been prime beneficiaries of the autocratic order are fighting back, directly themselves and indirectly through surrogates. The main argument of the critics is that the Executive Orders on the fiscal autonomy of the state legislature and state judiciary, and the LGAs infringe on the constitutional autonomy of the states. For instance, the Conference of Political Parties (CNPP), a coalition of 20 political parties views the president's move as a blatant violation of the nation's Constitution.

Some others, although not necessarily against the Executive Orders, believe that effecting the necessary changes may require a further constitutional amendment, which may be easy given the fact that Mr. President currently enjoys a cordial relationship with the leadership of the National Assembly. Opposing the propriety of the Executive Order is no less a person than the learned Sage

Prof. Ben Nwabueze who argues that Executive Order 10 is unconstitutional. He agrees perfectly that diversion or misappropriation by the State Governors of monies meant for their legislative assemblies, judiciaries, and local government councils are condemnable and call for firm actions to stop it. However, he opines that the outcomes that the Executive Order aims to achieve are already provided for in the constitution, what is needed is proper interpretation and implementation.

He notes that by making Executive Order 10, the President relies on the authority derived from Section 5(1) of the Constitution. But Section 5(2) avails the same powers given to the President in 5(1) to the state governors. And in no way does 5(1) imply that a President as head of the federal executive arm can lord over the state governor as head of the subnational executive arm. Moreover, the president in the spirit of the Nigerian constitution has no power to take over the functions of the legislature. With particular reference to the instructions provided in the Executive Order that the Accountant General makes direct deductions from the revenue accruing to the states for direct transmission to the state legislature and state judiciary, Ben Nwabueze argues that it is against the constitution to do so, as the Supreme Court had ruled against such an aberration in the past.

He notes that in the course of trying to solve a problem, which in this case is the state governors not placing the state judiciary and state legislature on the first charge while allocating revenues that accrue to the State, and not remitting the funds meant for the LGAs, the federal government should not itself be found guilty of what the governors are doing. Thus the federal government has to be cautious that in attempting to free the LGAs, state legislature, and state judiciary from the straggle hold of the state executive, it does not of itself strangulate the state governors because two wrongs cannot make a right. The autonomy of the state governments under the federal system flowing from the division of powers forbids and precludes that.

The position of Ben Nwabueze appears logical, but can hardly be deemed to be pragmatic. It may be considered as an exercise in legal romanticism and incapable of solving the problem at hand. If what the Executive Order seeks to achieve is already provided for in the constitution, then Mr. President merely reenacted it. Perhaps the aspect relating to the Accountant General making direct deductions may have to be expunged because it will bring further complications since the Governor remains the chief accounting officer of the state. Perhaps the Executive Order may have to stop at criminalizing violation of the constitutional provisions for the autonomy of the state legislature and state judiciary, and the LGAs, and not direct that the

Accountant General takes any action. But following the Executive Order anti-graft agencies may investigate violations and charge the Accountant General of states violating the constitutional provisions for misappropriation immediately, while the governor is charged after he/she leaves office.

Ben Nwabueze rightly observes that the governors are not acting constitutionally by not granting the other tiers and level the constitutionally granted fiscal autonomy. But he fails to say how the governors can be stopped from disobeying the constitution. He appears not to address the point that the governors are interested parties here, and are benefiting from not doing the right thing and that while it is true that the president and the governors are equals, but even in the animal kingdom, at least one animal (in this case the President) has to be more equal than the others, otherwise there will be anarchy, which certainly framers of the constitution did not intend. Nonetheless, it will be interesting for this and other executive orders to be interpreted by the Supreme Court to further deepen our democracy. But one thing is obvious, President Buhari has set the ball rolling and we hope to see more robust politicking henceforth in the states and the LGAs.

Sources

https://en.wikipedia.org/wiki/Buharism

https://www.vanguardngr.com/2019/02/the-movement-of-buharism/

https://www.ripplesnigeria.com/opinion-buharism-6-what-are-they-celebrating/

https://independent.ng/buharism-as-the-naira-collapses-so-does-nigeria/

http://saharareporters.com/2021/01/16/how-was-nigeria-buharism-ozodinukwe-okenwa

https://news.yahoo.com/nigeria-buharism-modernize-fast-154528771.html

http://www.gamji.com/sanusi/sanusi32.htm

https://sudanica.aminusumaila.org/uncategorized/buharism/

https://www.opinionnigeria.com/buharism-ideology-or-religion-by-abdulrahman-yunusa/

https://www.vanguardngr.com/2018/03/gdp-growth-deepening-poverty-nigeria/

https://www.vanguardngr.com/2019/11/how-epileptic-power-supply-is-increasing-poverty-unemployment-in-nigeria/

https://www.vanguardngr.com/2018/09/addressing-extreme-poverty-in-nigeria/

https://www.vanguardngr.com/2019/09/how-to-fight-poverty-in-nigeria-kpakol/

https://businessday.ng/opinion/article/nigeria-worlds-poverty-capital/

https://businessday.ng/politics/article/how-poverty-shapes-elections-in-nigeria/

https://punchng.com/is-the-recent-world-poverty-clock-assessment-of-nigeria-justified/

https://businessday.ng/opinion/article/poverty-and-widening-inequality-in-nigeria-2/

https://en.wikipedia.org/wiki/Presidency_of_Muhammadu_Buhari

https://www.thecable.ng/pdp-buharis-economic-policies-have-brought-nigeria-to-its-knees

https://www.premiumtimesng.com/promoted/465041-fact-sheet-the-buhari-administration-at-six-counting-the-blessings-one-by-one.html

https://www.thecable.ng/report-card-presidency-lists-buharis-achievements-in-six-years

https://nairametrics.com/2018/05/30/before-and-after-10-metrics-that-has-defined-buharinomics/

https://www.vanguardngr.com/2020/07/grave-consequences-of-buharinomics/

https://punchng.com/why-buharinomics-makes-me-nervous/

https://guardian.ng/business-services/the-four-year-buharinomics-so-much-so-little/

https://nairametrics.com/2021/02/25/buharinomics-in-stagflation-we-trust/

http://saharareporters.com/2020/08/18/failure-buharinomics-making-case-developmental-state-nigeria-babatope-falade-onikoyi

https://hallmarknews.com/world-banks-scorecard-on-buharinomics/

https://www.chronicle.ng/2019/02/10-facts-about-buharinomics/

https://thesouthernexaminer.com/buharinomics-and-the-poverty-of-nigerias-million-p2153-171.htm

https://www.thisdaylive.com/index.php/2019/01/18/buharinomics-new-book-on-buharis-management-of-economy-ready-for-launch/

https://ng.opera.news/ng/en/business/88f575d42641139c5d3f2fe9af0771b4

https://www.vanguardngr.com/2021/05/inflation-reduces-by-0-05-in-april-%E2%80%95-nbs/

https://gazettengr.com/buhari-an-incompetent-disappointing-leader-attahiru-jega/

https://guardian.ng/opinion/buharis-unguarded-tongue/

https://www.premiumtimesng.com/news/top-news/198259-buhari-didnt-refer-nigerians-criminals-presidency.html

https://www.commonwealthroundtable.co.uk/commonwealth/africa/nigeria/president-buharis-diplomatic-gaffes-and-negative-comments-abroad/

https://nairametrics.com/2021/06/09/how-buharis-high-political-risk-regime-could-hurt-nigerias-energy-investments/

https://library.fes.de/pdf-files/bueros/nigeria/10883.pdf

https://media.africaportal.org/documents/RP283.pdf

https://www.premiumtimesng.com/news/headlines/394155-buhari-signs-executive-order-on-financial-autonomy-for-state-legislature-judiciary.html

https://businessday.ng/opinion/article/president-buhari-and-local-government-autonomy/

https://en.wikipedia.org/wiki/Aisha_Buhari

https://www.bbc.com/news/world-africa-37642282

https://www.thecable.ng/who-advises-aisha-buhari-the-angry-matron-of-the-villa

https://guardian.ng/news/crack-in-presidency-as-aisha-buhari-lashes-out/

www.ingramcontent.com/pod-product-compliance
Lightning Source LLC
Chambersburg PA
CBHW050046260726
48658CB00005B/1801